CELEBRITY
SERVICE
BY GEOFF RAMM

First published 2015 by Creative Juice Publishing

www.geofframm.com

ISBN-13: 978-1502909930

ISBN-10: 1502909936

© Copyright Geoff Ramm

Book Design: Mark Moore, Purely Mint Promotions
Graphic Illustrations: Gabrielle Imerson, Public UK
Copywriter: Liz Hardy, Plays With Words
Helen Stothard, HLS Publishing Solutions

RAVING REVIEWS

"Even if you think you offer 5 star service, there is always room for improvement and this easy to read book will help transform your customer service ethos. Geoff through some great real-world examples is quite rightly challenging us to identify our competitive service gap and improve customer service to 'celebrity' status which will benefit the top and bottom line."
Phillip Singh - Vice President - Epsilon

"Geoff Ramm has done it again. His OMG marketing approach really helped me to change my view of how I promote my business a few years ago, and now his CELEBRITY service idea has just raised the bar again. A simple, elegant idea that everyone in your team will instantly understand, yet profound enough to impact your business strategy, Geoff delivers an important message in a punchy package. Highly recommended. It's already made a different to the way I approach my customers."
Dr Graeme Codrington - Co-founder and International director - TomorrowToday

"Hello. This is your business wake-up call and Geoff Ramm is here to kick start the action. Celebrity Service is a relevant, refreshing and witty read that could help take your service to another level. Do yourself a favour and put it at the top of your list. (Or go one step better and get Geoff to present to your team – it will be a session to remember!)"
Sharmila Nahna - Chief of Relationships – Ovations International

"Geoff knows how to capture an audience, whether it's during his interactive keynotes or through his books. He always delivers powerful, practical examples that are sure to inspire audiences to help them stand out from the competition through excellent marketing and service. Celebrity Service is a must read, it demonstrates how great service can stop you in your tracks anywhere in the world. The question you will be asking yourself after reading this is ... how do I measure up?"

Natalie Hudson - Marketing & Memebership Manager - VENUEMASTERS

"What I love about Geoff's work is that while everyone else is busy coming up with the latest interesting idea, Geoff has always moved on past that to the most difficult business of actually applying it and making it real in your business. Like OMG the ideas in this book are applicable to pretty much any business. They are based on an easily understandable but revolutionary concept and, if implemented, will transform your business... and indeed the world. Imagine an entire economy based on the idea of giving everyone in it Celebrity Service! Geoff is without doubt the funniest, most down-to-earth and most practical speaker and writer in customer service today. I urge you to buy this book and listen to the man speak!"

Caspar Berry - Motivational Speaker

"At last a book focussed on the true meaning of outstanding service. A great read and one that highlights that exceptional customer service is not dead. I have read many books about how to get the best out of customer facing employees but nothing provides such excellent referencing, true real life examples and a humorous relevant twist."

James Foice - Managing Director - ASAP

"Geoff Ramm proves that customer service is not a complex conundrum of convoluted issues requiring a cadre of committees to correct. Instead he brilliantly opens your eyes to an new perspective that gives way to a simpler solution that leads to amazing customer service."
Dawnna St Louis - Professional Speaker & Author

"What an absolute delight to read, Geoff's style is so brilliantly executed that you can instantly visualise the scene and better still you're transported there, hanging on the words, waiting to see what's happened. More than that though, is the use of examples which are things everyone can relate to and not the stock standard "safe" brands other people use when talking about marketing and customer service. Each example is brought to life with a real element of human brilliance. I found myself nodding as I read the pages, even laughing out loud, knowing I've been in situations like this or seen things like this happen! The Celebrity Service examples can't fail to make you smile, and leave me wondering how I can usurp my customer's expectations!"
Lissa Balmer - International Trade Advisor - UKTI

"YOU PROBABLY THINK YOU DELIVER GREAT SERVICE,

BUT THEN A CELEBRITY WALKED IN... AND EVERYTHING CHANGED!

GEOFF RAMM, CELEBRITY SERVICE SPEAKER

Dear Ms Armour, Ms Young, Ms Ramm and Ms Cornell,

We are delighted to welcome you to the Apex Waterloo Place hotel. We trust you will enjoy your stay with us.

Please accept my sincere apologies that we had to rearrange your treatment times on Sunday 3rd November 2013 due to one of our therapists calling out sick and that one of these time changes was unsuitable leading to the cancellation of your treatment.

Thank you for being so understanding about this matter. Please find enclosed a drinks voucher by way of apology as well as this gift bag as a good will gesture. I would also like to offer you 10% off spa treatments (subject to availability) on your next visit. Please see my card attached with my contact details in order that I may organise this for you for next time you are in Edinburgh.

May I also take this opportunity to say Happy 40th Birthday Ms Armour! Enjoy your stay.

Kind regards,

Karoline Watts
Front Office Manager and Yu Spa Team!

WALNUT STREET Supper CLUB

FOREWORD

The subject of customer service, or customer experience as it is increasingly known, has been the subject of numerous books over the years, many of which I have bought, several of which I have actually read!

They range from the enduring classics by the likes of Ken Blanchard, to complex body language analysis, Neuro Linguistic Programming, and psychological mapping of behaviour. Often these books are intellectually engaging and thought-provoking, but the concepts they describe can be very difficult to execute across the frontline of an organisation. That's not because staff on the frontline can't understand the concepts; it's because in successful organisations staff on the frontline are usually too busy and distracted to spend time working out how to apply them – too busy serving customers!

By contrast this is a simple book, written in simple language that makes it easy to read, and central to the book is a simple concept that is easy to grasp. In all my years at John Lewis and with the many organisations I have consulted for since, the simple ideas were, almost exclusively, the most effective.

The idea of Celebrity Service taps into a dominant and growing culture that has been in existence since the beginning of the last century and continues to grow annually – just look at the reality TV programmes: X Factor, Britain's Got Talent, The Voice, and of course, in business, The Apprentice. Everyone can immediately identify with how they might treat their favourite celebrity and how that may currently be different from how they treat their day to day customers.

Couple a simple but effective concept with some wonderful illustrative stories, and Geoff is a great storyteller, and you have a book that could make a real difference to your organisation. I hope you enjoy reading it as much as I did.

Andrew McMillan - Former National Customer Service Manager, John Lewis
Principal at Engaging Service • www.engaging service.com

CONTENTS

**To the people
who put a smile
on every customers face,
I thank you.
Your service will
never go unnoticed...**

Dedicated to Hayley, Grace & Elliot x

"The Queen thinks the world smells of paint".

Billy Connolly

ALSO AVAILABLE

If there was a 6th star on the rating.......

........I'd have lit that up as well!. I've read plenty of marketing books in my time and they're all awash with great ideas but all too often great ideas cost great money! This book is fantastic! Easy to read (literally two facing pages to each chapter) you don't even need to try to get into it, it just happens! The only problems you'll have with this book are 1) putting it down and 2) your mind being blown with the possibilities.

5 out of 5 stars Completed within 48 hrs.

... couldn't put in down! Wowzers, one of the most digestible books I have EVER read... on anything. Its a book I will be going back to many, many times. For all you creative nuts, BUY IT! For all of you who dare to be different BUY IT! If you don't even know if you're part of the boring sea of sameness, then definitely BUY IT!

5 out of 5 stars OMG Observational Marketing

A breath of fresh air, real marketing for real people. A book with practical tips and help for business, without the jargon. This is a brilliant book and should be in everyone's office as a reference. This book is from someone who has practised what he preaches, an inspirational marketing person.

OMG:
WHEN YOU
COME ACROSS
SOMETHING SO
AMAZING THAT
YOU JUST HAVE
TO TELL THE
WORLD!

BORN OUT OF FRUSTRATION

My love and passion for marketing is well-documented in my first book, OMG (Observational Marketing Greats), and although as a child I remember great marketing, I must confess I can't recall my first time of receiving great customer service. So at what age do we start to remember customer service?

I believe it's when you start to earn your own money and take home that first pay packet. With that hard-earned money in your pocket, you now have the ability to choose where you spend it. As you hand over your cash, you're entering into a transaction which comes with a series of expectations – you pay for your purchase from the vendor, and in return you expect a great product, a smooth process, and excellent service. Maybe it's because you are wiser to what is going on, or maybe when you start making your own way in life you appreciate how much you've had to work to be able to afford cars, holidays, clothes and groceries, but by this stage I think what we all expect, as a bare minimum - is good service. As a business you may not be able to fight your way to number 1 on Google; you may never be able to compete with large-scale advertising campaigns; you

may never reach the dizzy heights of a social media viral sensation, but there is one thing you can always compete for (and win) - the hearts and minds of your clients and customers.
The only way to achieve this is through outstanding customer service. In an ever-changing business world where competition comes from online, the high street, overseas, and no doubt in the future outer space, this is the one true competitive differentiator for you and your team.

So why is it that as a husband, a dad, a businessman, and a professional speaker, I am becoming increasingly frustrated by poor service? What disappoints me more than anything are the barriers, the rules, the red tape, and the sheer doggedness that stops me, you, and many others from being happy with the service we are receiving.

The longer I myself am a customer, the more I notice a frequent unwillingness to delight. Surely this should never be the case!

There are countless books, manuals, training courses, customer service gurus, online and on-the-shelf resources, just waiting to be explored, digested and used, but how many of these ideas and service concepts are taken onboard and willingly delivered?

I am known for my Observational take on the marketing world, but for many years I have also observed the world of customer service with a magnifying glass and fine-toothed comb. While half of my business is focused on helping businesses and audiences gain more clients, the other half is concentrated on helping businesses to upgrade their customer service beyond that of the competition - to become memorable for all the right reasons.

So, it is with my Observational eye that I am bringing to the fore a different way of helping you to look at your service; a way in which you, your team, and your business can improve every conceivable customer touch-point in your organisation.

People kill brands, people kill service, and people have the power to break or make your reputation. NB: For 'people' see: team, partner, cleaner, maid, chauffeur, receptionist, call centre, distribution, driver and, yes... YOU!

Poor service delivered by anyone in your company gives your customers fuel to ignite a flame with the potential to destroy your business. You have been warned!

There are hundreds of books on customer service, focusing on what you - the CEO, director, executive, business owner or entrepreneur - can do to revolutionise your team, organisation or business. Flick through the pages and you may recognise some of these phrases; give yourself a gold star if you do...

Delight your customer! Go the extra mile! Exceed expectations! Treat the customer how you wish to be treated!

Sound good? Sound familiar? It all sounds rather bland and same-old, same-old for my liking. This is the sort of material I read back in University and College. What does it really mean? If you were to repeat these mundane phrases to your team, would they really be inspired to make the difference?

Is this it? Is this the answer to incredible word-of-mouth reputation building? Is this the answer that leads to customers beating down your door and queuing overnight to get in?

No, which is why I've become increasingly frustrated.

For all the CRM software and data developments, there has never been a seismic shift in how customers are served. We're not using the information available to us to come up with creative ways to out-smart and out-serve the competition.

So the time has come, to say 'enough is enough'. It is time to think differently. It is time to inspire your team with a new outlook, a new vision, and a work environment where common sense and independent thought are at the heart of decision-making. The aim is to improve each and every customer touch-point, and service experience at every opportunity.

If you've come here expecting chapter and verse in service psychology, you will be deeply disappointed. However, if you are looking for **ONE BIG IDEA** to invigorate you and everyone around your business to think differently and to find the gap your competition can't touch, this book is full of ideas to inspire it! There is no guarantee, but this one book may just hold the answer to propel you to your competitive edge, and the answer may well be easier than you think.

There is a new way of customer service thinking, and like Father Christmas on the 24th December, it's exciting, it's full of surprises, and it's on its way to be delivered by your business.

PLEASE DO NOT READ

(it will only make you angry....)

The immortal line .. *"Don't make me angry, you won't like me when I am angry"* - came from the lips of Dr David Banner when sheer frustration would turn to anger, and then into rage, and within minutes a mountainous green creature would emerge, swiftly followed by a visit to the tailors.

What you are about to read are 100% true stories.
Every one of them had me turning green - not with envy, but with a Hulkesque rage!

FIRST JOB:
YOU'VE BEEN WARNED

Having graduated from Sunderland University Business School I spent over a year posting CV's (yes, this was a while ago now) trying to plant my first foot on a career ladder with the name marketing attached to it. In-between sending CV's and speaking to recruitment agencies, I had to take a job to help contribute to the mortgage and bills, so I manned the telephones of a gas and electric utility company.

I won't go into too much detail, but hasten to add that we were one of the darlings on the BBC Watchdog programme most weeks, with a reputation for underhand sales and service techniques. It was during this time that the gas and electricity markets were de-regulated and it seemed that some salespeople were going out of their way to sign up anyone they could, by any means necessary, in order to grab that all-important commission.

Unsuspecting customers would receive a letter on their mat explaining that they were going to be leaving their current supplier, and would very soon be switching over to us!

You could imagine the emotion of the callers when they rang to complain (and rightly so). Irate customers demanding to stay with their current supplier and not to be switched. Sadly, we had to tell them that it was too far into the system and that this switch was going to happen, regardless. An awful job, an awful way to treat customers, and a sharp welcome to start my career in the big world of real work.

I don't remember her name, but I do remember the crying down the line of an elderly lady who was in tears on the telephone, saying she didn't want to switch, and that she must have been duped at the doorstep.

She was in such a state, and I tried everything I could to help calm her down and to help her, but a few taps on the keyboard confirmed my fears –
she was coming to us, regardless. I said to her that I'd call her back and would do my best to stop this from happening.

Her reply:
"Will it be this week?";

"It will be in the next hour", I said.

She didn't believe me, so I gave her my personal extension and told her to ring me at any time. I rang back within the hour and told her the bad news. She'd stopped crying by now, and then she completely shocked me...

"For all your help and honesty in calling me back I will stay with you...can I keep your number?"

From an old-aged pensioner crying down the phone, to someone who was now happy to stay - I was both amazed and delighted.

Of course, all incoming and outgoing numbers and calls are monitored, and the following day I was called into the Manager's office. I was looking forward to telling her what had happened and the amazing customer u-turn the day before, but before I could speak I was receiving my very first, and ultimately, last, verbal warning. The reason? For giving out my extension number, a move which was against company policy and The Rules.

It was at this point that the essence of this company's customer service hit home. It simply did not exist. Being nice or, indeed, doing the right thing to make a customer happy was behaviour that merited punishment and reprimand. What more can I say?

One week later, I left... I had found the first rung on my career ladder marked **'Marketing'.**

THE HUSBAND: HANGING ON AT THE END OF THE WEDDING

We hired the photographer, videographer, the cars, venue, bought the favours, flowers, and everything else you could imagine. We hired the menswear and bridesmaids' dresses, but bought the dress – please remember – we bought the dress.

The day after the big day we were off on our honeymoon, so I asked my parents if they could take the hired clothes back to the bridal shop to reclaim the deposit. We returned from honeymoon to find that all of the hire clothes were actually still at home. I rang my parents to see if everything was alright, and they explained that they had returned everything, as we had requested, to the bridal shop, but they had been told the deposit couldn't be returned due to a missing clothes hanger.

When they had taken the clothes back, the shop assistant behind the counter was making wedding small talk and had asked for the bridal dress clothes hanger. The hanger was not there. The hanger for the dress - that we had bought, remember - was not there! The upshot to this minor incident was that we could not get the money back until the shop had the clothes hanger back in their possession.
We hunted high and low, but with all the upheaval of the wedding, we could not find it. Eventually we gave up the search, went back to apologise, told them we could not find it, and finally - very begrudgingly - we were given our deposit back.

We had spent a small fortune with that business, and this minor detail spoiled the entire experience which had, up to this point, been brilliant.
Years later we moved house, and as we were moving boxes... we found it. Now I know what you are thinking – the hanger must have been gold plated? Laden with diamantes? Or perhaps diamond encrusted? Not quite. To see this exquisite work of art for yourself, turn to page 116. Once you've picked yourself back up off the floor, come back here...

Our photographer for the big day was very good; a bit pricey, but good, and umpteen albums were purchased by our families after the big day. Years later, we received a letter from him saying that 'Due to their growing success, they have too many negatives taking up too much room and are therefore going to have to throw them away to free up some space'. Rather than pop them in the same envelope and say "but we thought you'd like them at no cost", the letter continued with: 'If you would like them before we bin them they are available to you for an amazing £50 extra'.

We were the first of our close friends to get married. We spent months researching venues, visiting suppliers, and emptying the bank account to find the so-called best-of-the-best for our big day. Naturally, when the time came for some of our friends to be married, they often asked us for our recommendations. We gladly gave them, but not for the photographer, and not for the bridal shop.

People who put rules and greed before putting a smile on your face will puncture their business until it becomes flat. The customer who you've served poorly will never recommend you, but will undoubtedly talk about the negative experience they had with you.

MERCURY RISING

A few years later, on the 1st March 2002, I started up my own business called Mercury Marketing. Like all sensible people, I did a bit of research before I launched.

I took to the phones, pretending to be a member of my target clientele - entrepreneurs and small to medium enterprises - calling to ask marketing companies what services they offered, how much they charged, etc.
(I must warn you that this was pre-Google, and some readers may find the following sentence alien or somewhat disturbing). I reached for the Yellow Pages, and contacted every marketing company in the region… there were 11 in total.

The following results have been ingrained in my mind since 2002…

• 3 companies simply rang out, with no answer machine,

• 3 said they did not market entrepreneurs/SME's (2 actually laughed, thinking it was beneath them),

•2 companies said they would ring me back (I am still waiting, but as the eternal optimist, I am sure it will be any day now),

• 2 said they would send some information (like an excitable puppy, I am still looking out for the postman with a packet from one company. The other did appear, but the quality of the materials and print was truly awful… homemade, at best),

• 1 said he was writing a book on marketing and, when it was available to buy, I should buy it!

So here I am posing as a potential client, and not one person helped, advised or encouraged. However frustrated I felt at the time, I was equally happy that this was the competition I was about to face…

Game On.

THE COUPLE: WHEN JIM BOWEN MET GOLDILOCKS

Way back in the 1980's there was a hugely popular trivia gameshow on UK television called Bullseye, hosted by Jim Bowen. A mixture of the pub game/sport of darts and general knowledge, it was a show that spawned many a catchphrase, but one in particular was "Look at what you could have won". This was frequently said to the losing couple at the finale of the show if they had failed to score 101 or more with their 6 darts. The curtain would open to reveal a fitted kitchen, a Vauxhall Nova or, more likely, a speedboat!

Some years ago we spent the weekend in Stirling, right in the heart of Scotland - a beautiful place, rich with William Wallace history. We left our hotel room at a well-known hotel chain, had breakfast, and took an early morning stroll. When we came back we walked towards our room and could see a chink of light at the end of the corridor. "The cleaners must be in there already", I said. We walked in and there on the bed was the cleaner... asleep!!! (aka Goldilocks). I walked gingerly in and quietly said "Hello?". Nothing; she was flat out. "Hello?", I said, a little louder, now. On the third, much louder attempt, she awoke, startled. She shot up out of bed, brushed herself down, and started to clean the room. We said *"it's okay, the room is clean"*, and asked her to leave.

We spent the next 24 hours in shock.

Sleeping in our bed like Goldilocks was only half the story, so where does Jim Bowen fit in? We came back later that day and decided we needed to inform the management, not wanting to get the girl into trouble, but they needed to know what happened. They thanked us for telling them. 24 hours later we finished breakfast – ironically with porridge and checked out. On checking out the manager said, *"Thanks for letting us know, and we are really sorry for what happened yesterday"*. He foolishly continued, *"It's a shame you complained later in the day as we could have given you last night for FREE, but the computer says we can't now."*

Look at what you could have won!

In the most stupid of stupid circumstances, we were at fault for complaining "too late", and the manager did not have the authorisation or common sense to override the computer.

Is there anything more frustrating than knowing a computer is ruling your decisions, regardless of what is right or wrong?!

THE DAD:
SITTING ON THE FENCE?

Two panels of our fence came down due to high winds, making the back garden far too dangerous for our two young children to play in. With 2 less-than-impressed kids, we had to act fast.

Calling on recommendations from friends and a few firms from a local magazine (the one they paid to be in to attract work!), appointments were made over the phone, to measure up and to then provide a quote.

One company never sent the quote as promised.

The company we chose, decided not to call us back to start the work.

Our second choice arrived a week late and took two weeks longer than expected (as they had double-booked the diary).

Is this it? In one of the biggest global recessions ever recorded, I can only assume that the stories in the press are nothing but a smokescreen/media hype, as it appears no-one who we called needed the business.

TERRIBLE TWOS

"Wait until you reach the terrible twos" is a phrase often wheeled out by friends and family to strike fear into the minds of unsuspecting parents of babies...
Tempers, tantrums, and refusing just about everything are the general rules of thumb. But no, this is not about Elliot, who has just turned two; this is about two companies who believe being awkward, stubborn and irritable is the correct way to behave.

For his birthday, we bought Elliot a combined wooden seat and sand pit. It arrived from the online store in time for Mr McGivor Ramm to assemble it. After two hours of building, and like a blast from the 1980's furniture past, there was a screw fixing missing - one that would ensure the structure was safe for the kids to play on.

Disappointed at 20:45pm – yes! But fear not, I went online to this rather large and famous brand, and emailed customer services using their online form (particularly mentioning the fact that I needed a replacement fixing in time for his birthday – you know those Any Other Details boxes that seem to go unnoticed?).
There was no email response the next day, so I rang up...

The response...
"Oh sorry we can't send you out a replacement part. Although this product is ours, you purchased it from (think of the largest toy retailer you can think of and you probably have the name), so you need to contact them." So I did.

The response?
"Ah, we can't open another box and send you this part. However," and here's the good news,
"It's a generic fixing so I would advise you to go to your local DIY shop, purchase one, and we'll refund you for the fixing." So I did.

2 large DIY chain stores and 1 independent shop later... "Sorry, this is a specific part for this product; you'll need to speak to them." So I did.

"Oh, unfortunately this product is now SOLD OUT. The best we can do is to order the part for you from..." wait for it... "POLAND!"

The first email was sent in May 2014 (I still have not had a response), at the time they said they would order the part and post it to me. When I rang back for the final time, the customer services person read back all of the previous conversations and the promises that had been made (another really great CRM system which means nothing when no-one takes control to solve a customer issue), but still didn't offer a solution.

I also took to Twitter to report the service and seek help – no response! I live in hope that this elusive fixing will arrive soon.

Feel free to email me at geoff@geofframm.com for the screw update and I'll tell you if it has arrived.

CHUFFING KEYS

To celebrate Elliot's birthday, we decided to take him to a theme park which has a famous toy brand attached to it (we thought it would be better than a half-built sand pit). The plan was to book a themed room (months in advance) so on the morning of his birthday he'd wake up to toys, cake and balloons in his themed bedroom.

We travelled four hours by car and duly arrived at the check-in desk, and couldn't wait to see the looks on Grace and Elliot's faces, as we'd kept this a secret surprise for them.

"Good Afternoon Mr Ramm..."

"Good Afternoon."

"Ah, has no-one contacted you?"
"No. Should they have?"

"There is a problem with your themed room. You can't have it."
"Okay. So can we have another themed room please?"

"No, they're all booked."

At this point I let off more steam than the hotel could carry!

"What we can do is put you in a standard room at a reduced rate."
Insert a barrage of discontent with the reception staff holding their ground, a manageress who had left and could not be contacted, and knowledge that the secret surprise was ruined. I was fuming.

For over 45 minutes we exchanged our views and we had to stand our own ground to get the very best out of the problem. We settled on an upgraded room that night, and had a great day in the park the next day. Having eventually spoken to the manageress the next morning, we stayed for an unplanned second night in the themed room and really did have a great time.

So what could have been done differently?

They should have called us!

They should have looked at the Any Other Requirements box (are these boxes meant to be ignored?) that said this trip was for a child's birthday.

They should have made suggestions other than a downgrade.

They should have apologised!

And what was the problem with the room we had booked?

The electronic locks on the doors had broken.

Can we go back to things called "Keys"!!!
When the football, rugby or cricket team is on a poor run, the boss, manager or coach will stop and go back to basics - running, passing, shooting, catching.

Get the basics right and you are on your way.

Business is just the same. Keep your customer updated at all times, have a better response than anticipated, and stick to what works.

All of these examples could have been avoided with simple common sense.

After every example I asked myself one question... What if?

What if I were someone deemed more important - would I have got the deposit back without the hanger, first time?

What if I were deemed more important - would I have received the photograph negatives for free?

What if I were deemed more important - would Goldilocks have stayed out of our bed, and would we have got the 2nd night free in the hotel?

What if I were deemed more important - would the fence have been quoted for and repaired on time?

What if Elliot was the son of someone more important – would he have been in his themed room and had a complete, safe toy on his birthday after a new fixing had been delivered on time?

If only I, we, us, were more important.

COME IN No TEN
YOUR TIME IS UP!

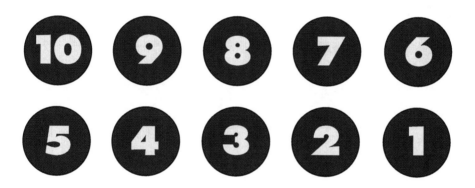

Answer truthfully - On a scale of 1 to 10 how would you rate your overall customer service right now? 1 being truly awful, 10 being incredibly amazing.

If you marked yourself 1-4, you know you have an awful lot of work to do; if you are 5-8 then you know you could be doing better. Even if you are confident enough to choose a 9 or a 10, I know you can easily improve every aspect of your service further.

Many scales end with 10 - 10 being the highest mark possible - but are there numbers beyond this for you, your team, and your business?

You see, we all believe we are delivering constantly high levels of service, but what I am about to reveal is the game changer. It will shift your entire mind-set to how you deliver service in future.

WHY CELEBRITY?
WHY NOT
★ ★ ★ ★ ★
SERVICE?

Five star has always been the pinnacle of service standards, but what if you or I were to visit a 5 star establishment and receive 5 star service and then a celebrity walked in – there would, again, be a difference in attitude, delivery and persona.

The world famous 7 star hotel, the Burj Al Arab in Dubai shows clearly how five stars, just like any number, can always be superseded.

It's widely known that a Celebrity does not have to do much to be offered the best seat in the house or secure the best table in an already full restaurant.

Celebrity is greater than 5 Star. It top trumps its status. It is reserved only for royalty and Hollywood A-Listers. It was probably best summed up in 1990 when Miss Vivian Ward entered a Hollywood boutique and was shown the door moments later, due to her inappropriate dress at the time. Oscar nominee, Julia Roberts, played the part of Miss Ward in Pretty Woman. For those of you who haven't seen the movie, she walked into the same store a day later wearing a more conservative, expensive outfit and uttered the lines: "Big mistake. Big. Huge.", and swiftly left the store, leaving the sales assistants wishing they had provided Celebrity Service to all their customers.

Of course this is just Hollywood, right? Wrong!
Before launching my own business in 2002 I was a marketing manager of a motor retail group in the UK,

marketing and promoting some of the world's most iconic brands: Honda, Chrysler and Toyota, to name just a few. My main objective was simple - to encourage you to take a test drive. A salesperson would then take over with the aim of converting the sale.

Our good friends were in the market for a new car, a sporty 2-seater. I made them aware of the new Toyota we had at our Durham branch and told them it was ready for a test drive. They went to the branch that Sunday morning.
When I next spoke to them I was delighted to hear that they had purchased their brand new sports car and it was going to be delivered in one month's time. But, they didn't buy if from our dealer! They drove a further 30 miles to another garage and purchased the new car from them!

What the...?!

When they had arrived in Durham they asked to test drive the car, but the salesperson said that wouldn't be possible. The dealership was tight on space, so numerous cars would need to have been moved, and as the salesperson was short on time, energy and colleagues that morning, he said that they could not test drive it that day but to come back soon.

I was furious. One person's lack of service led to the main competitor securing a great sale.

"Do what you do so well that they will want to see it again and bring their friends."

Walt Disney, Founder of Disney

"Kind words can be short and easy to speak, but their echoes are truly endless."

Mother Teresa

SATISFACTORY SERVICE? SATISFACTION GUARANTEED?

You and your customers will only ever remember Celebrity Service or Shocking Service... the term 'Satisfactory, or satisfied' will never be memorable and falls into the whatever /average trapdoor of unremarkable people and brands!

In fact, it's not worth wasting the ink on these pages for, so let's move on...

WELCOME TO THE BIRTH OF
CELEBRITY SERVICE

It's not something I sat down, thought long and hard about, or created; in fact the term Celebrity Service appeared out of nowhere during a talk I did at a conference in the UK some years ago.

This half day event was split into two, the first half was all about marketing ideas and how businesses could gain customers and clients by standing out from the competition. There was a short coffee and comfort break and the second half featured a host of customer service ideas and stories on how to retain customers.

As the MC introduced me back onto stage, for some reason I completely changed my planned opening line, and said: "Do you treat all of your customers in the same way?" In an audience of around 300 people, roughly half of the room nodded their heads, apart from one woman who was sat near the front. She shouted out, "Absolutely, Geoff!" I was taken aback – as was the rest of the audience; she was so adamant and so animated. I replied "Wonderful, you treat every customer with the same high level of standards each and every day, not matter what?" "Yes", came the answer. "What sort of business do you have?" "I run a boutique store selling children's toys, homeware and kitchenware, all made out of wood, metal and stone. It's very exclusive and rather expensive".

"This sounds great, now give me examples of how you deliver great service all of the time?

"We serve tea and coffee."

"Wow, how much?"

"It's complimentary."

"What else do you do?"

"We have comfy chairs in the store so people can sit and browse before buying."

And then I paused... and from nowhere asked her the question that was about to change everything.

"Okay, but what if a celebrity were to walk into your store tomorrow?"

"Like who?" she replied.

I was caught on the hop! So said, "Do you like men or women?"

"Men."

"Okay, think of an A-List...

Celebrity… Hollywood… Male… Movie… Hunk…"

She thought for a few moments (with a wry smile on her face) and then shouted out two answers……

"George and Brad" (you know how hunky you are when you don't need a surname!)

"So, picture the scene, George Clooney is making a movie in this area, he's been here for 6 months and is flying back to the United States tomorrow, but before he goes he wants to buy some gifts for his family. He's heard all about you and your store and wants to come in and buy. However, he's tired. He's tired of the paparazzi and tired of signing autographs. So he phones you up and says…

"Hi there, I'm George Clooney, I want to come to your store tomorrow but I'd love to have some privacy away from autograph hunters and paparazzi, would you mind closing the store for me, please?"

So I asked this lady sat at the front of the audience "Would you close it for George?"

"Oh yes", came the reply with an ever-widening smile.

"Great. Now I am staying here tonight and I am speaking at another event tomorrow, would you close the shop for me?"

She remained silent and ever so slowly shook her head from side to side…

Cue 299 people raising their eyebrows and in a split second one embarrassed lady put her hand over her mouth and let out a gasp "Ooh………I would treat customers differently."

"That's okay, I would expect that, but, what else would you do for George tomorrow morning?"

At this point most of the audience laughed. The lady thought about it and to everyone's amazement, including mine, she came up with half a dozen ideas in just thirty seconds!

These were the answers I can recall from that day:

"I'd get my hair done" (she mentioned her sister was a stylist)

"I'd wear my best dress"

"The wooden floor has needed varnishing for at least 6 months – I'd do it tonight" (See Billy Connolly quote on page 15.
And the last idea was the real shocker………

"I'd get rid of the tea and coffee".

"What?!"

"Yes, but I'd bring in proper coffee".

Half a dozen ideas in 30 seconds, based on a celebrity hypothetically entering her business. She said she was already delivering the highest possible service, and then a celebrity walked in… and changed everything about her attitude and mind-set on service.

Quite simply there is a gap in your customer service you never knew existed and Celebrity Service will stretch that gap to leave your competitors in its wake.

(as illustrated by a recent audience member in her business…)

CELEBRITY SERVICE

¡Thank you Geoff!

'BRAD PITT' SERVICE

this is the tool for me to communicate my vision!

STANDARD 'EXCELLENT' SERVICE

"The customer experience is the next competitive battleground."

Jerry Gregiore, CIO, Dell Computers

"Your most unhappy customers are your best source of learning."

Bill Gates
Founder of Microsoft

CELEBRITY

*Late Middle English (in the sense 'solemn ceremony'):
from Old French celebrite or Latin celebritas, from
celeber, celebr- 'frequented or honoured'.*

To help you explore the concept of
Celebrity Service in more detail I've
broken it down into bite size chunks;

- **Consistency**
- **Excitement**
- **Love**
- **Engagement**
- **Bravado**
- **Independence**
- **Thank You**
- **You and Your Team**

Each area looks at the standout
brands and people who deliver
"Celebrity Service". Whether you are
a Celebrity or not would make very
little difference in what they said,
what they did, or how they reacted.

If you think of the wondrous sights and sounds of South Africa, you probably think of Table Top mountain, Kruger Park, or maybe Spion Kop. For me, I make a beeline for one place, and one place only: my favourite petrol station in the world.

I first wrote about Alison and her chalkboard sign outside her BP garage in the OMG book, and revelled in how creative and cost-effective this one idea had become. It's one of my all-time favourite stories, and can also be viewed on my YouTube channel. You see, for over 40 years, Alison and her family have written a message, joke, quote, or quip on the board, to put a smile on motorists' faces along Jan Smuts Avenue in Johannesburg.
This is not only genius marketing, but what I am about to reveal is the reason why I have included her (again) here... No matter what

happens in your business, consistency is the key to service delivery.
In December 2013, one Facebook post left a lump in my throat.

It was the day Nelson Mandela died and for the first time Alison put down her chalk and hung a black veil over the sign as a mark of respect. During the mourning period every message she wrote was a quote from the great man and former President.

It was a wonderfully touching thing to do, and a small yet clever mark of respect.

Months later I returned to South Africa (avoiding the tourist sights and sounds) and headed out to see Alison and the board again.

To my dismay, everything was closed. The forecourt was dug up, diggers were strewn everywhere, and a high

metal fence perimeter was erected.
The business was shut.

But not the sign.

Here is what I snapped:
Is there anything worse than
inconsistency in customer service?
Where you never know what to
expect from day to day? This one
example proves that no matter what
state your business may be in, you
should never give up in consistently
pleasing the customer.

FOOTBALL IS 90 MINS OF PRETENDING YOU'RE HURT
RUGBY IS 80 MINS OF PRETENDING YOU'RE NOT

INSPIRATIONAL IDEAS

"The goal of the company is to have customer service that is not just the best but legendary."

Sam Walton, Founder of Wal-Mart

Can you name a member of cabin crew from any of the flights you've ever taken? Possibly, but more probably not. Over the years, an incredible amount of publicity has justifiably been given to the wonderful service on-board South West Airlines in the United States, and by now, like me, you've probably watched many viral videos they have featured in.
There was no video camera to capture this trip, but what I am about to share with you is quite simply the greatest cabin crew member of all time.

She brought excitement to the passengers in just 90 minutes.

I'd just finished speaking at a conference in Harare, Zimbabwe. Having arrived at the airport, I quickly received my boarding card.

Glancing at it I was mildly excited to see I was sat in 1F. I'd been upgraded! (I was wearing my 3 piece suit after all).

Now, I have a lot more confidence in larger planes than I do smaller ones. We were called to our gate and walked onto the tarmac. But there was no plane to be seen, only a tiny aircraft with propellers in the distance. Yes, this was our plane. On the horizon, huge black clouds started to engulf the city and the sounds of rumbling thunder and the odd fork lightning flash lit up the skies. I was becoming nervous thinking by the time we board the plane the storm would be upon us. I walked up the stairs and was met by two cabin crew.
"Good afternoon, sir, can we see you boarding card?"
"Yes, certainly" (but I could not find which pocket in my suit I'd put it in).
"Oh, we do apologise Sir..."
"No that's okay, here it is".
She paused, looking at my upgraded ticket, and then she lent in and whispered...
"Oh... you have won a prize!"
"What have I won?"
"I can't tell you now, but I will soon".
I walked a few short steps and took

my seat beside an older gentleman (the propelled plane was so small we were in Economy!). I turned to the gentleman and said;
"Did you win a prize?"
"Yes, but she wouldn't tell me what it was." At this point the row across the aisle turned to us and said that they had also been told they were prize winners.

Being sat at the front gave me a great vantage point as I could hear every single conservation as the rest of the passengers boarded. What struck me was that everyone received a compliment, and I mean everyone. Whether it was about their clothes, hair or even about the toys being carried by children as they boarded with their parents.

Everyone was buckled in and we started to taxi. The cabin crew member then picked up the phone and announced to everyone that she was delighted everyone was on board and then proceeded to say – "And you have the best looking cabin crew serving you today", with a sarcastic smile.

She asked very politely if everyone would take out of their front pockets the safety instructions and read them, as it would really help us all should an incident occur.

I looked around and for the first time ever – everyone did! The phone was put down and she leant into the first row aka the prize winners and said:
"Here's your prize,: you have just won the chance to help me open the door should there be an emergency". Well, we all fell about laughing.

We'd been in the air for 30 minutes and the drinks trolley came through. As First Class/ Economy front row passengers we were first up. She served the gentleman to my left:

"Would you like a drink sir?"
"Yes please, a water".
"Would you like ice with that?
"No thanks."
"Oh you're way too cool for ice..." Again we raised our eyebrows and laughed at this engaging yet exciting service.

Half way back to South Africa I took the short walk to the front of the plane and spoke to her and told her that what she did from take off to now has been brilliant and that she indeed gives great Celebrity Service. Ladies and gentlemen meet Christina (left), she works on AirLink a part of South African Airways. Celebrity Service – the ability to provide customer service to everyone, not just celebrities.

INSPIRATIONAL IDEAS

*"If you work just for the money,
you'll never make it,
but if you love what you're
doing and you always put the
customer first,
success will be yours."*

Ray Croc, Founder of McDonalds

It would have been rather an easy 'L' to have chosen Loyalty within the Celebrity breakdown.

Loyalty, of course, is brought on by great service wrapped around a great product or brand. The next step would then be advocacy, personified for me by the Apple brand. Meet an iphone, ipad or mac user and you'll come across an advocate born out of loyalty for the product and its support.

Where else in the world would you receive high fives from the staff as it opens its doors to a new store or launches a new product?

'L' in celebrity is quite simply Love. As Lennon & McCartney wrote:
"There's nothing you can do that can't be done.
"Nothing you can do but you can learn how to be you in time - It's easy."

You simply have to love delivering fantastic service. Not just in the great times of *'nothing is wrong'*, but also when the blame is on you, when you have made a mistake, and when things just aren't going according to plan.

APEX HOTEL, EDINBURGH
4 ladies, 40 candles, and 1 capital.

The weekend was planned months in advance; a chance to celebrate a friend's birthday, free from the Husbands, enjoying some pampering beauty treatments, and the chance to lie in without little ones bouncing on the bed at 5am.

However, on the train on the way to the capital 3 of the 4 ladies received a call on their mobiles explaining that their previously booked spa treatments would need to be re-arranged due to a member of staff ringing in sick that day. The ladies were all naturally disappointed as the weekend had been planned to the minute, however the hotel said they would sort something out upon their arrival. As promised, upon arrival the group were met with a huge apology and given the time to go through the system to make sure another suitable time slot could be arranged.

2 of the 3 booked for treatments were able to go ahead with another time, so not an ideal situation but it had been well handled and so the group were able to just move on to the next part of their planned weekend.

The story doesn't end there however, as when the ladies went to their rooms later that day to drop in their luggage they were met with a personalised note and a goodie bag of gifts as an apology for any disruption, a display of sheer love of service.

When it goes wrong, we put it right, not just with an apology but with an offer, but not just with an offer, but with a further discount, and a goodie bag (whatever that may be), and a letter, card or note that is personalised. Natalie at the Apex in Edinburgh gets it. She has independence to make these decisions and does the right thing.

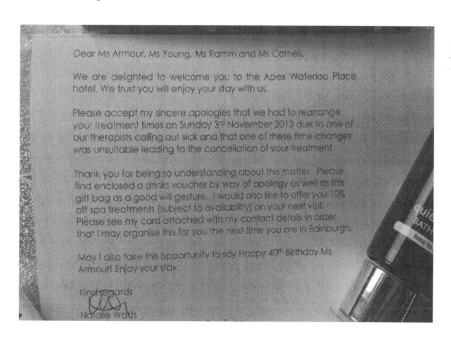

Dear Ms Armour, Ms Young, Ms Ramm and Ms Cornell,

We are delighted to welcome you to the Apex Waterloo Place hotel. We trust you will enjoy your stay with us.

Please accept my sincere apologies that we had to rearrange your treatment times on Sunday 3rd November 2013 due to one of our therapists calling out sick and that one of these time changes was unsuitable leading to the cancellation of your treatment.

Thank you for being so understanding about this matter. Please find enclosed a drinks voucher by way of apology as well as this gift bag as a good will gesture. I would also like to offer you 10% off spa treatments (subject to availability) on your next visit. Please see my card attached with my contact details in order that I may organise this for you the next time you are in Edinburgh.

May I also take this opportunity to say Happy 40th Birthday Ms Armour! Enjoy your stay.

Kind regards

Natalie Watts

RADIO STAR

I've been a long-time advocate that service will forever lead to the sale. The salespeople that serve, win, and it's as simple as that!

Back in my days of being a Marketing Manager, along with direct mail, website, press and exhibitions, radio advertising played a big role in our marketing strategy. As soon as I was appointed, my name and picture were in the local paper, and within days the radio sales reps swooped to connect with me, craving a meeting.

There were four local radio stations at the time, each stating they were the biggest, had the largest reach, or the biggest catchment for our demographic. One after the other, laptops were opened, PowerPoint presentations were played to demonstrate their superiority, and then the reveal of the rate card where the salesman/woman would discuss prices. Every one the same, every one putting themselves before the client.

In walked David Lee, from Metro Radio. My office was at the back of the room so I noticed that as he came in he was handing out CD's of new and established artists they had had that month in the studio. My team were delighted. There was no laptop. No rate card. It was a coffee and a chat – not about Metro, but about me and what I wanted to achieve in my role.

My answer was the same as it's always been – to create ideas that no-one else will think of, and to make commercials that will stand out from the crowd. The conversation naturally turned to football and then back to what I wanted, and the rest, as they say, is history.

On the back of the interest shown in the team and me, I commissioned my first campaign with them. It was not to be the last.

We were all invited to football matches, received tickets for shows and cinemas, and the sweets/candies and CD's were always arriving out of the blue. Reading this you may think it's just corporate schmoozing, but from the first encounter, David put service in front of any sale.

Several months later I happily recommended a very large utility company to use David to advertise their staff recruitment days. He got the contract.

He loved to delight, he loved to listen, he loved to help, and he loved his work.

INSPIRATIONAL IDEAS

**"The more you engage
with customers, the clearer
things become and the easier
it is to determine what you
should be doing."**

John Russell, President of Harley Davidson

ENGAGEMENT

Engagement has been one of the buzziest of buzz words in marketing and service for some time now (and rightly so), but what I want to challenge you with is not only engaging the customer who holds the purse strings, but to seek out opportunities to engage their nearest and dearest too.

Our favourite family theme park in the world has to be Portaventura in Spain. The attractions are for all ages, the weather is always great, but it's the little things for the little ones that make this place so special.

Customer Service starts well before you even get into the room. For the first time we'd booked a themed room – a Woody Woodpecker themed room, to be precise. The concierge welcomed us to the hotel and parked up our car whilst we took Grace inside to the special themed room check-in desk.
We sat down and before we could say who we were and how many nights we'd be staying, the lady behind the desk said to Grace, "Oh, I have something for you...

Woody asked me specifically to give this to you when you got here". Grace's face was beaming at this point as the lady reached down, opened the drawer of her desk, and pulled out a plush Woody Woodpecker soft toy.

We then started to check-in, and throughout this process between the grown-ups, the lady frequently paused to speak to Grace or to ask her a question.

"That's it", she said, *"Woody has just told me your room is ready, and later on you can see him in the park, and, of course, tomorrow morning for breakfast. C'mon lets go..."* As she got up she held out her hand to Grace and the pair of them walked together out of the lobby with us following behind. We went up in the tree lift (a lift painted to look like a tree) and were led to our room – Grace was shown in first, of course. Once we were in there were more gifts, including a bathroom set which she still has to this day.

Take a trip to Birmingham International train station in the UK and if you look down you'll come across this wonderful service engagement for canine travellers. Whether you are travelling first class, standard, on or off peak, Virgin Trains provide fresh water for their canine customers before they board the train.

On the subject of our four-legged friends, a good friend from my college days, sadly had to say goodbye to her 15 year old West Highland White Terrier. She said her final goodbye and a few days later received a sympathy card from the veterinary surgery… the card and the pre-printed words was probably enough, but what tipped it into the Celebrity category was the power of the written word, and the time and effort taken to comfort the customer.

Dear Rachel & family

The foot prints left behind may fade but in your heart they will always stay

So sorry you had to let Holly go today. She was a fantastic wee dog who'd obviously had a great life.

Hope you're ok,

Lots of love,

Wendy & all the girls at
King's Road Vets

Hats off to Premier Inn, Derby West, for engaging / hooking the attention of Grace and her friend once they entered their family hotel room. Sitting on the bed were two little plastic yellow ducks on top of a note, which read....

Moments later they were running down the hotel hallway (faces beaming) and into the reception area.

They were met by one of the most welcoming reception staff I've ever seen, who became as giddy as the children as she reached for the 'tasty treats'.

Great creative ideas like this don't cost the earth, but they engage our nearest and dearest, which sets the tone for a great experience with that brand.

Now what could you do?

Hey Guys!

You found us..........Well done!

Our names are Daisy & Donald. If you take us back to the reception team here at Derby West Premier Inn we will reward you with tasty treats in return!

Enjoy your stay!!

INSPIRATIONAL IDEAS

"We see our customers as invited guests to a party, and we are the hosts. It's our job every to make every important aspect of the customer experience a little bit better."

Jeff Bezos, CEO of Amazon

Picture the scene: 11:30pm, a cold night in Edinburgh, Scotland. I was on my way to see the Edinburgh Fringe Festival from my hotel near the Haymarket. On the way back I passed a bike shop (push bikes rather than motorised) called The Bike Smith. By now the shop must have been closed for 5 or 6 hours; the shutters were down, there was no contact number, no help sheets outside, and no-one around, and yet they were still providing service! But how?

Take a closer look at the image... they simply chained up a large foot pump and left it outside for any cyclist who needed extra air in their tyres!

Would you risk having something stolen to ensure you were serving your customers out of hours? This was not only brave, but a genius service idea.

EXCLUSIVE LTD

Are you confident in the service your team provides? I mean really, really confident? For award winning Recruitment and HR Consultancy firm Exclusive Ltd they have implemented a customer excellence programme which monitors candidates' and clients' perceptions at every touch point of their recruitment journey. Feedback is posted on their website, in the same way that reviews are posted on TripAdvisor, so any level of feedback can be seen by the public at any time. It certainly keeps all team members on their customer service toes.

Would you be brave enough to do the same?

A PERSIAN PROMISE...

Back in November 2009, I embarked on my very first trip to Iran to speak at the World Advertising & Branding Forum. Our plane landed into Tehran airport at 1am, and was followed by a further 1hr drive to the hotel.

As soon as I was in the car, I switched on my phone to text home to say I'd arrived safely. There was nothing! No signal, no nothing! But that's okay, I'll phone when I get to the hotel room.

2:30am, I tried calling home, but after many attempts at dialling a variety of numbers, it would still not connect.

3:00am decision made to open up the laptop, connect to the internet and email / send messages via social media. You know where this is heading now... Countless attempts, and no successful connection.

Now worry had turned into mild panic: this call was important and needed to be made.
3:15am I got into the lift and headed to the reception desk. I spoke to the concierge and explained my situation; *"Ahh, no problem Mr Geoff, I shall connect you through our telephone"*... Yep, you guessed it, we could not connect.

3:45pm Mild Panic had progressed to Moderate Hysteria.

"Please, Mr Geoff, I will look after this for you. I promise! Please give me your wife's email address and I shall email her for you."

"Are you sure?"

"Yes, I promise. And if she emails you back I will print it out and let you see it straight away."

4:00am the sun is rising and I get my head down for 2 hours' sleep.

Now imagine your partner is away for the very first time on the other side of the world, and they had promised to let you know they had arrived and, more importantly, that they were safe. Then you received the following email:

**Dear Mrs Geoff,
We have your husband.
Do not worry he is safe.**

A promise is a promise, and Hotel Persian Evin certainly delivered, perhaps not in the carefully crafted words we would have liked to ensure comfort and security, but they did what they said they were going to do. Luckily I was able to get in touch with Hayley the next day to reassure her that I really was ok!

INSPIRATIONAL IDEAS

_____

_____

_____

_____

_____

_____

_____

_____

_____

_____

_____

_____

_____

_____

"It is not the employer who pays the wages. Employers only handle the money... It is the customer who pays the wages."

Henry Ford, Founder of Ford Motors

Whenever I think of the word Response in customer service I can't help thinking about the 'You must pick up the phone within 3 rings!" scenario.

However, forget 2 rings, 3 rings or a whopping Olympic-sized 5 rings, this form of response concentrates on the art of how you can respond: not with time, but with technology, and how you can stand out from the crowd by personalising whilst surprising your customers.

There's a BMW Mini garage just a mile from our home, which we pass most days in the car. Outside of the showroom, for everyone to see there is a bright pink (think Lady Penelope from Thunderbirds) Mini Cooper.
Of course, no-one would buy it, it would surely depreciate very quickly, but it certainly turns heads... one head in particular is Grace's.

Grace loves the car and had been asking to go to see it for some time. As luck or bad luck would have it, Hayley's car had just broken down and she was in the market for a new car. Days later Hayley and Grace went to the showroom, saw a car they liked, and Grace got to take a closer look at her little pink dream.
Details were exchanged and the saleswoman from BMW Mini said she would send out further information. Hayley came home expecting the usual car-sales collateral to be sent out, maybe a folder with inserts and prices of the car, a DVD, or an email with pictures and further details.

None of the above materialised; what she promptly received was a video email which the saleswoman had recorded on her phone or camera, going into greater detail as she filmed around the car.

Now at this point I need to stress the quality was not great, it was taken ninety degrees on its side, the sales pitch could have been so much better, but this did not matter – this was different, this was personal, and this made Hayley feel special.

Response is not just the time you take to respond, but with the exciting technology at our disposal we can respond in a different, and in a highly personalised way.
However, the real element of 'Celebrity Service' was still to come. A second email pinged onto the laptop, from the same woman, featuring a second video made just for Grace, featuring the bright pink Mini.

Celebrity Response is not just how fast you come back to the customer, but how creative you are in doing so.

How could you respond using similar technology? There are many forms of online video facilities to choose, but for now check out Eyejot which is free and will help you personalise and deliver in a way your competitors have yet to think of. The answers to improving your service are there, we just need to be inspired to do so.

LOST LUGGAGE, LOST BUSINESS

With the aim of shopping for a good carry-on case for short haul flights I walked into a store not far from me in a retail outlet village. Having picked up a couple of cases I asked the 2 staff members which size was allowable on planes.

"We don't know" was the abrupt reply from one, whilst the other said, *"Every plane is different so you'll never know which to take unless you know the carrier you are flying with"*.

And with that, I left the store.

There was another luggage shop in the retail village. I walked in, found the case I liked, and asked the same question.

"Ah," said the lady, *"let me show you this..."* She took me to the front of the store, removed a large case from the shelf, and there behind it was a size chart for different carriers, detailing what they would and would not accept as hand luggage.

A different service, aided by knowledge and aided by the fact they had answers ready for this type of question.

What questions are you regularly asked? What questions could you be asked? Do you have the answers ready for anyone who comes to you? I bought 2 cases from that store, the smaller hand-held and a larger case for a few nights away. They were on buy-one-get-one-free. I've recommended the shop ever since.

It's easy to sell when you help.

"Be everywhere, do everything, and never fail to astonish the customer."

Macy's Motto

INSPIRATIONAL IDEAS

For some, Customer Service is written up in a rule book for staff to follow.

But in the world of 'Celebrity Service' there are no rules; it's a blank canvas, where the answer invariably starts with 'Yes'.

Being a fan of American Football, I went for a tour of the Lincoln Financial stadium, home of the Philadelphia Eagles. Having stood pitch-side, sat in an executive box on the 50 yard line, and checked out the locker rooms, I proceeded to the store and as well as a jersey, soft toy eagle, and a shiny Eagles helmet, I bought a sun visor hat for Hayley. Back at the hotel whilst looking through my purchases I noticed the electronic tag was still attached (I have no idea how I got through the security doors).

Not having time to go back to the stadium, I entered a clothes store in downtown Philly but they could not remove it as they didn't stock it. The second store was the same. At this point and on my third attempt I felt like the big bad wolf, and, cap in hand, I entered Macy's department store. Within moments the shop assistant had removed the tag and even put the visor in one of their bags! Like the others, she did not have to as they did not stock this item. But you have to ask yourself the golden questions - would the first two stores have helped me had I been Johnny Depp? Yes – and there's your gap!

ROARING PUBLICITY

If you wanted to respond to a disappointed customer, what would you do? Give them a freebie? Offer a future discount? Or simply put a smile on their face?

Through radio stations and social media I came across one such disappointed customer. Bill Bennett made a cheeky request to a customer service adviser that he wanted a drawing of a smiley dinosaur. And this was exactly what he received.

Mr Bennett then took to the internet to proudly display the drawing, and it went viral.

The story began when he wrote to retail giants Marks & Spencer, asking for a refund after he was mistakenly charged £3.00 for a £1.90 salmon sandwich at a store in Taunton, Somerset.

He received a reply offering him a gift card, but a few weeks later it had still not arrived, so he wrote again – asking for a 'hand-drawn picture of a smiley dinosaur' to compensate 'for the inconvenience'.

He expected his request to be ignored. But Steve Jones, a customer adviser who seemed to share Mr Bennett's sense of humour, sent him a £5 gift card, the sketch, and a note reading: 'Please also find a picture of a smiling dinosaur, hand drawn.

Unfortunately art was never my strong point, but I hope you will appreciate it. It's a wonderful story that with social traction can help brands reach out to a vast audience with their acts of wit, cheek, or humour.

WATER WORKS

Richard Searles has worked for utility giant Northumbrian Water for over 22 years. He's a mechanical engineer by trade, and is now Customer Contact Manager.

When I heard about the level of independence their engineers and sewerage teams have alongside the call centre I knew I just had to meet him to find out more.

He told me they have over four million customers reaching from the Scottish borders, Cumbria, Yorkshire, and down to Suffolk.

Of course these are a different kind of consumer – they can't swap suppliers unless they up sticks and move. Nevertheless, Northumbrian Water is regulated by OFWAT and every quarter, research is conducted to benchmark their customer service.

Get it wrong and fines are there to be received! On a scale of 0 – 5 Richard explains we always aim for a 6. We know it's impossible to achieve a 6, but we may just hit the 5. Richard explained: *"At Northumbrian Water we have what is called "Our Way" which is our own cultural change programme. As part of "Our Way" we have what is called "Our Gift To You",* where, as a team, if we think we can help with a problem or see the opportunity to delight, we will take it. For example if the company makes a mistake or leaves a mess, etc. the sewerage worker or distribution technician on site has the independence to make a decision to speak with the customer service call centre to offer a gift. But they don't just call to order the standard bottle of wine or chocolates; when they call they will share a personal observation about the customer, including if they liked fishing, or if they were celebrating an anniversary, or if there's a new baby in the house."

To help Northumbrian Water stand out from other service providers, their gifts are ordered and sent to the customer as a surprise. Books on fishing, or a hamper, or baby products are sent as a random act of service.

They collaborate with a local gift company in Darlington who distribute the gifts, but what was interesting to hear - there is no financial cap on the gifts.

Every member of the team has the authority to see the opportunity to delight the customer and to send the surprise.

How independent are your team and organisation? Are there rules to stop such service?

INSPIRATIONAL IDEAS

"Our mission statement about treating people with respect and dignity is not just words but a creed we live by every day. You can't expect your employees to exceed the expectations of your customers if you don't exceed the employees' expectations of management."

Howard Schultz, CEO Starbucks Coffee

The business has been done and you appreciate the fact that your customer or client chose you. You would of course thank them straight away, but take note, the 'Thank You' in Celebrity Service also stands for the after care and keep-in-touch ideas that can continually delight, surprise, help, and inform.

First, ask yourself this fundamental service question – who has thanked you for your business recently? I am not talking about the 'thank you' message on a receipt or a 'thank you, please call again' sign, I am talking about genuine appreciation or a random act of kindness after you have made a purchase.

Attending the Paralympic Games in the Olympic Stadium in London was simply one of the greatest days out we have ever had. The Olympic stadium on the morning of Day 4 was packed with pure inspiration, so imagine my delight when I met face to face the Blade Stunner herself, Stef Reid.

I told her what an inspiration it was and that we actually saw her medal in the long jump at the Olympic Stadium. I said Grace was in awe and it was a day she'd remember for the rest of her life. Stef then said *"Thank you for coming to see us"*, and *"what's your address? I may have a little something to send Grace."*
A week later a limited edition set of Adidas Paralympic Game sunglasses arrived together with a signed note from Stef.

It may be a little easier saying thank you from one person to another, but what would you do if you were a global player in the telecoms arena?

To thank me for my business, Carphone Warehouse sent the following box, and inside was a bar of Lindt chocolate.

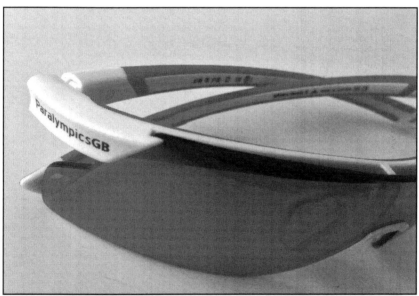

INSPIRATIONAL IDEAS

**"There is only one boss.
The customer.
And he can fire everybody
in the company from the
chairman on down simply
by spending his money
somewhere else."**

Sam Walton, Founder, Wal Mart

...Philadelphia. It was midweek, and outside the streets were being pounded by heavy rain as we ventured out for a meal and a few drinks. Around half of the restaurants were closed, and the ones that were open were sparse, to say the least.

All except one: The Walnut Street Supper Club. Inside, it was packed to the rafters, bustling with atmosphere, and we were fortunate to be given a table right in front of a small stage and piano.

Whilst we were ordering drinks, the pianist jumped up to the stage, sat down, and called out one of the singers' names. She hurriedly ran to the stage and proceeded to belt out a flawless song.

Another singer got up 5 minutes later, and then another. What I found incredible was that these were not professional entertainers. They certainly didn't look like entertainers.

They were the waitresses and waiters. Whilst not serving, they each sang their hearts out to the customers. It was a brilliant night in which I saw a full team working as one to deliver exceptional service.

By 11:30 pm there were just four of us left - myself and my good friends Corey Perlman, David Newman, and Jay Baer. As the last ones standing we were treated to an encore by all of the staff.

It wouldn't have mattered had we been Tom Cruise, George Clooney, Brad Pitt and Johnny Depp; they brilliantly delivered Celebrity Service and we loved it, we spoke about it, and, as you can see, I wrote about it.

Why should it just be your service department that delivers service? Celebrity Service flows through everyone, from CEO to office junior, from Managing Director to the lavatory cleaner. Watch the video on my YouTube channel to see the final encore from that great night!

STUNT DRIVE EXPERIENCE

June 15th 2014 and a wonderful surprise gift on Father's Day... James Bond, Jack Bauer, Jason Bourne, eat your heart out... I was going to become a stunt driver for the day!

We all travelled down to the family-run business Stunt Drive Experience in Stockton, where I was to learn how to donut a BMW Z3, and hand-brake turn and parallel park a Mini at high speed.

As we entered the cabin to hand over our gift vouchers and to sign in, we were welcomed by a lovely lady, Jane Bird. Along with another 13 drivers with their partners and children, there must have been 30-plus people helping themselves to tea, coffee, biscuits, and squash. Once everyone signed in, we walked outside to the stunt driving briefing, led by Paul Bird – one of the most charismatic and quick-witted people you are ever likely to meet.

He was joined by his daughter, Kelly Bird, Sarah Hall, and Brian Jukes. All five of them gave the safety briefing, and then did something pretty special...

They asked everyone, including the non-drivers, to say their name and introduce themselves to the rest of the group, so we did. After each person the Stunt Drive team would all shout out 'Hello Geoff', all the way around the circle. We got round the whole group, and then it happened. They announced that they were going to go around the group and remember every person's name. And they did! Everyone was amazed, everyone felt special, and it set the tone for the next few hours.

Remembering someone's name is one thing, but 30 in a row? That is something special, and is just one of the ways in which they deliver Celebrity Service.

98

INSPIRATIONAL IDEAS

"Loyal customers, they don't just come back, they don't simply recommend you, they insist that their friends do business with you."

Chip Bell, Founder of Chip Bell Group

TELL THE TRUTH

ANSWER, TRUTHFULLY, THE FOLLOWING QUESTIONS:

Proposals:

Q. A potential client has asked for a proposal from you. How long does it take you to write and send it?
A. A day, a week, or longer?

Q. How would you deliver that proposal?
A. Email (saved as a pdf), Posted 2nd or 1st class, or express courier?

NOW LET'S INTRODUCE 'CELEBRITY SERVICE'...

Angelina Jolie asks for a proposal from you...

Q. How long does it now take to deliver that proposal?

A. My guess is her proposal will have made it to the top of the pile, sitting in front of everyone else's. Possibly everything in your office or workshop will stop until it is done.

Q. How would you deliver it?

A. I think you can forget about emailing or using a post-box; if it's possible I'd place my bets that you would deliver it by hand. It would be printed on the best paper you could lay your hands on, and quite possibly your car would be cleaned en route to accentuate the wonderful suit or dress you were wearing.

The simple concept of a Celebrity Service proposal would make a big impact on every one of your customers. So what will you do, starting from today, to raise your client care to Celebrity Service?

Your business is closing for the day.

Before the shutters come down the phone rings. You let it go to answer machine, and hear that the customer has a problem.

Q. Do you rush back to pick up the call to help? Do you visit that customer to help put the problem right? Or do you wait until the morning to call back?

Q. Johnny Depp leaves the message. Do you do the same as above? Or do you pick up and go straight round to fix the problem?

"Customers don't expect you to be perfect. They do expect you to fix things when they go wrong."

Donald Porter, VP of British Airways

HOW TO USE
CELEBRITY SERVICE?

FOUR COLUMNS for you and your team to discuss, debate, and improve upon every customer service touch-point to help take you from good to Celebrity...

TOUCH POINT	CURRENT SERVICE

If you are struggling to think of an A-List movie hunk or goddess then here are a few to help you on the next page...

CELEBRITY NAME	IMPROVED SERVICE

CRUISE
MURPHY PITT
GOSLING
FORD MCGREGOR
MOORE CROWE
CONNERY
GIBSON KNIGHTLEY WILLIS
HANKS PALTROW
PORTMAN CRAIG
SCHWARZENEGER
THERON JOLIE

LAW FREEMAN
BALE
WATSON
ANNISTON STALLONE
FERRELL
DAY LEWIS JACKMAN
WASHINGTON BERRY
BLOOM AFFLECK
ROBERTS JACKSON
HOPKINS
DE NIRO STREEP
CARREY

HOW TO SPREAD CELEBRITY SERVICE IN YOUR BUSINESS

You get the simple yet effective method of Celebrity Service, but how will others in your department or business adopt this way of thinking?

You Will Need: Celeb magazine, glue, scissors and picture frame

Step One:
Each staff member of the department chooses their own Celebrity Hunk or Goddess, they print them out, or cut them out, and they frame them to their hearts content.

Step Two:
Everyone strategically places the image near to them when they are connecting with the customer e.g. by the telephone, computer, reception desk, staff room, locker or in their vehicle.

Step Three:
After every interaction a glance to the image is enough to make everyone think... if this was this person, what would I do?

What they are creating is a visual reminder of the person they need to think of before every email, face-to-face, social media touch point to help them scale greater heights when needing to out-serve the competition.

**"You are allowed to do this....
don't worry about the rules,
don't worry about getting
into trouble, your job is to
take care of the customer.
Your job is to make the
person leave happy."**

John Pepper, CEO and Co-founder of Boloco

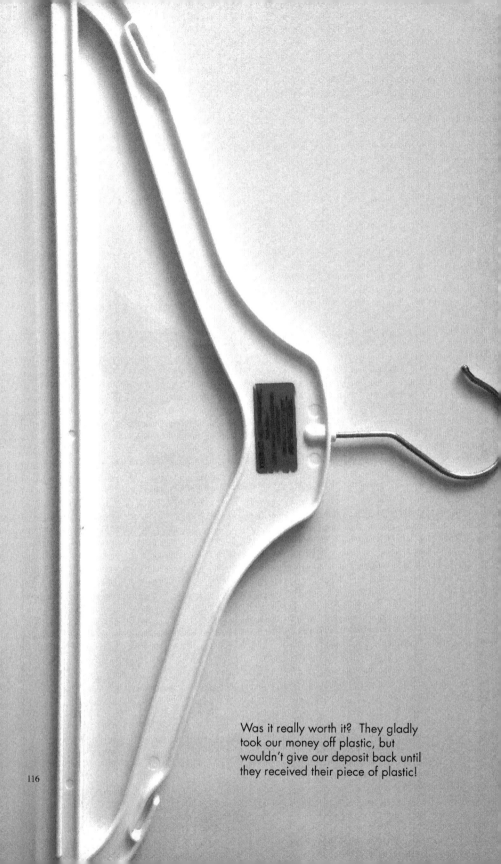

Was it really worth it? They gladly
took our money off plastic, but
wouldn't give our deposit back until
they received their piece of plastic!

SAINT

This is how Grace is welcomed into the Hamleys toy store in London. How do you welcome your customers as they enter your business?

WE ASK GUESTS TO

KINDLY REMOVE

THEIR SHOES

BEFORE WALKING

UP THE STAIRS

THANK YOU

SINNER

And this is how I was welcomed
into a hotel recently ....

SAINT

This flower shop in Kish Island was simply stunning. Magnificent displays caught the eye and attracted you into the store....

SINNER

But sadly, this is the person
who would be serving you today.

d, medium
r and smooth

ee choice,
anced.
e your own
by combining
y coffee.
creamy nutty
offee

REFRESHMENTS

Your visits are important to u
While you are here, please choo
from the selection below.
If there are any refreshments no
the list that you would like for y
next visit, please let us know

SAINT
OBC Accountants giving you a
numerical advantage over your
choice of refreshments

SOFT DRINKS

Classic full
Kenya.
flavour, fresh
nd Malawi.
ffeinated – A
affeine gently

Orange juice
Lemonade
Diet Coca Cola
Mini Coca Cola

Water

COMPANY POLICY

ue to our company policy we regret that

ll customers coming into the restaurant

will be charged for the buffet whether they

have anything from the buffet or not.

Sorry for any inconvenience this may cause.

. The Management

122

SINNER

This was the biggest sign on
the window of this restauarant...
Is it any wonder business' struggle?

SAINT

The staff of the Downtown Marriott, Philadelphia wore a welcome NSA badge for the duration of the 4 day conference, making sure all 1300 attendees felt welcome

poo and divi   spectator ↑

Studios 1 and 2 ↑

Meeting rooms 1 and 2 ↑

SINNER

You can have an Olympic sized
swimming pool but attention to detail
will leave you drowning with the rest.

Through these doors wal

he loveliest people in Fulwell

'And you're one of them.

SAINT

If you are going to praise your
customer... Do it like Barclays
Highly visible on the High Street..

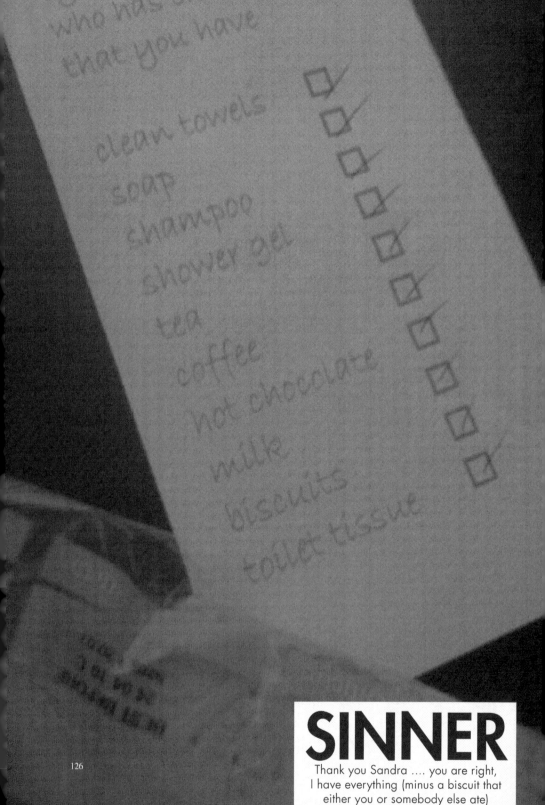

who has che...
that you have

clean towels ☑
soap ☑
shampoo ☑
shower gel ☑
tea ☑
coffee ☑
hot chocolate ☑
milk ☑
biscuits ☑
toilet tissue ☑

SINNER
Thank you Sandra .... you are right,
I have everything (minus a biscuit that
either you or somebody else ate)

WISH YOU WERE HERE

They say leave the best til last...and the best for me is simply proof that the Celebrity Service technique works.

It can inspire, it can galvanise the team, and it will create the gap in customer service the competition can't touch you for...

It all happened on the wonderful Mediterranean island of Malta. EC English Language Centres is a very successful business, which prides itself on having high levels of customer service and positive feedback from their pupils and agents.

They teach English to over 40,000 pupils a year in their 18 schools throughout the USA, Canada, UK, Malta and South Africa.

On the 8th April they asked me to speak at their Senior Leaders and Marketers Conference, to help further inspire their customer service thinking and delivery.

On arrival I was met at the airport at 1am by the taxi driver, Nunzio (below). On the journey to the hotel I found out that he'd worked with EC since they began in 1991.

He was knowledgeable, friendly, but, most of all, passionate. He is the person the pupils meet for the very first time when they travel from all over the world to study English in Malta. It was a wonderful few days working with the team, and by the end everyone was whipped up to thinking differently whilst upgrading every touch-point to a Celebrity Service standard.

I certainly wasn't expecting a call just one month later, from EC asking me to come back to Malta, this time to deliver a keynote and interactive workshop for their admissions and sales teams. I touched down at 2:30am on Friday 6th June. Nunzio was not there this time, but a colleague was, along with a very impressive sign which was waiting for me...

A VERY WARM WELCOME TO MALTA, GEOFF RAMM!
From The EC Sales Team ☺

In just 6 weeks, EC had designed a brand new welcome sign by upgrading from the simple display of a corporate logo to a montage of photos of their teams in Malta, as well as a personalised message at the bottom. At 2:50 a.m I was met by Alexander at the desk at the Valentina hotel in St Julians. *"Before I check you in, I just want to welcome you to the hotel"*, and then he reached out his hand and shook mine! Now there's a first. Having looked on TripAdvisor I noticed they were number one – I said I was looking forward to staying at the #1 rated hotel in Malta... his reply: **"Ah yes, we are number 1 right now but we must always keep pushing!"**

My room was on the fourth floor. After a delayed flight, and with an early start the next morning, I needed to hit the pillow, fast! But not tonight. As I walked in, I was met by constant surprises!

Orange (EC branded colours) balloons were at the foot of the bed, a pair of "I Love Malta" flip flops sat beneath them.

On the bed was an Orange (of course) towel, a nursery rhymes book, and an orange glass ornament in the shape of a snail, hidden underneath the pages of the book. Beside the desk area and alarm clock was a box of Yorkshire Tea, biscuits, sweets, chilled drinks, fruit, a chicken and mushroom Pot Noodle, and further chilled drinks in the fridge!

I filmed the experience and posted to YouTube – type in Geoff Ramm Celebrity Service EC English Language Schools to watch.

Now every pupil who chooses EC receives a personalised welcome board and gifts galore in their rooms when they arrive.

This was a Celebrity Welcome which took just a matter of weeks to permeate throughout the team, and one which will continue to raise the bar and help them to stand out from the competition. They understand the concept, they bought into the idea, and are creating ideas they never thought of.

KEEPING UP WITH THE KARDASHIANS

Whilst speaking at the Goldwell conference in Shanghai, I challenged the salon owner managers to upgrade their current level of service to Celebrity Status. Imagine my suprise when I received this email from Wildlife Hair Company who had taken Celebrity Service one stage further... Enjoy!

Dear Geoff,

My wife Jayne and I were at the Goldwell seminar you spoke at in Shanghai and had a blast. We both liked your Celebrity Service section and thought we should bring it back to our team. Rather than just re tell your story we decided to put it into play "for real". We have a monthly joint staff meeting for our two salons with approx 30 staff at the meeting. Kim Kardashian is doing a tour of Australia and next week she has an appearance at Westfield Shopping Centre. Our staff were all aware of the trip and one had even entered a competition to meet her. I told them that we had been asked to do the hair for Kim and her entourage as she hated getting her hair done in a hotel room and our salon has wonderful views of Sydney harbour and the bridge. At this point I had one young member of staff ask me if I was joking, "Do I look like I am joking?" I answered and she had to leave the room to "compose" herself. I then listed the conditions on our powerpoint bigscreen

• **5am Start**

• **Everybody has to wear white**

• **Only Kanye music to be played**

• **Fresh Flowers and Fruit**

• **No Talking to Kim or her entourage**

• **Top secret so no social media etc**

I had half the staff put their hands up to be there at 5am dressed in white, another two were putting together a Kanye playlist and someone was going to the markets for fruit and flowers on the way to work.

Point made.

Thanks for the idea.

Gary and Jayne

Wild Life Hair, Sydney, Australia

www.wildlifehair.com

THE
END
FOR NOW?

So there you have it, from singing waitresses, to the greatest cabin crew in the skies, a bicycle pump which stays up all night just for you, to the personalised video of a car you are thinking of buying, Celebrity Service can stop you in your tracks at any time, leaving you with the greatest feeling for that person and that brand.

It will forever be the person delivering Celebrity Service who drives the brand, and never the brand driving the Celebrity Service experience.

What will you improve from today? 10 out of 10 is just the starting block to propel your service to another level; that level is where you will find the gap you never realised existed.

WISHING YOU EVERY FUTURE SUCCESS.

To book Geoff for your next conference or to watch more celebrity service moments

Email: geoff@geofframm.com • Website: geofframm.com • You Tube : Geoff Ramm

GEOFF RAMM WILL RETURN IN OMG STRIKES BACK

Made in the USA
Middletown, DE
07 May 2017